# DREAMS

## HENRI BERGSON
### (1859-1941)

### TRANSLATED, WITH AN INTRODUCTION, BY

## EDWIN E. SLOSSON
### (1865 – 1929)

# CONTENTS

INTRODUCTION DREAMS

## INTRODUCTION

Before the dawn of history mankind was engaged in the study of dreaming. The wise man among the ancients was preëminently the interpreter of dreams. The ability to interpret successfully or plausibly was the quickest road to royal favor, as Joseph and Daniel found it to be; failure to give satisfaction in this respect led to banishment from court or death. When a scholar laboriously translates a cuneiform tablet dug up from a Babylonian mound where it has lain buried for five thousand years or more, the chances are that it will turn out either an astrological treatise or a dream book. If the former, we look upon it with some indulgence; if the latter with pure contempt. For we know that the study of the stars, though undertaken for selfish reasons and pursued in the spirit of charlatanry, led at length to physical science, while the study of dreams has proved as unprofitable as the dreaming of them.

Out of astrology grew astronomy. Out of oneiromancy has grown—nothing.

That at least was substantially true up to the beginning of the present century. Dream books in all languages continued to sell in cheap editions and the interpreters of dreams made a decent or, at any rate, a comfortable living out of the poorer classes. But the psychologist rarely paid attention to dreams except incidentally in his study of imagery, association and the speed of thought. But now a change has come over the spirit of the times. The subject of the significance of dreams, so long ignored, has suddenly become a matter of energetic study and of fiery controversy the world over.

The cause of this revival of interest is the new point of view brought forward by Professor Bergson in the paper which is here made accessible to the English-reading public. This is the idea that we can explore the unconscious substratum of our mentality, the storehouse of our memories, by means of dreams, for these memories are by no means inert, but have, as it were, a life and purpose of their own, and strive to rise into consciousness whenever they get a chance, even into the semi-consciousness of a dream. To use Professor Bergson's striking metaphor, our memories are packed away under pressure like steam in a boiler and the dream is their escape valve.

That this is more than a mere metaphor has been proved by Professor Freud and others of the Vienna school, who cure cases of hysteria by inducing the patient to give expression to the secret anxieties and emotions which, unknown to him, have been preying upon his mind. The clue to these disturbing thoughts is generally obtained in dreams or similar states of relaxed consciousness. According to the Freudians a dream always means something, but never what it appears to mean. It is symbolic and expresses desires or fears which we refuse ordinarily to admit to consciousness, either because they are painful or because they are repugnant to our moral nature. A watchman is stationed at the gate of consciousness to keep them back, but sometimes these unwelcome intruders slip past him in disguise. In the hands of fanatical Freudians this theory has developed the wildest extravagancies, and the voluminous literature of psycho-analysis contains much that seems to the layman quite as absurd as the stuff which fills the twenty-five cent dream book.

It is impossible to believe that the subconsciousness of every one of us contains nothing but the foul and monstrous specimens which they dredge up from the mental depths of their neuropathic patients and exhibit with such pride.

Bergson's view seems to me truer as it is certainly more agreeable, that we keep stored away somewhere all our memories, the good as well as the evil, the pleasant together with the unpleasant. There may be nightmares down cellar, as we thought as a child, but even in those days we knew how to dodge them when we went after apples; that is, take down a light and slam the door quickly on coming up.

Maeterlinck, too, knew this trick of our childhood. When in the Palace of Night scene of his fairy play, the redoubtable Tyltyl unlocks the cage where are confined the nightmares and all other evil imaginings, he shuts the door in time to keep them in and then opens another revealing a lovely garden full of blue birds, which, though they fade and die when brought into the light of common day, yet encourage him to continue his search for the Blue Bird that never fades, but lives everlastingly. The new science of dreams is giving a deeper significance to the trite wish of "Good night and pleasant dreams!" It means sweet sanity and mental health, pure thoughts and good will to all men.

Professor Bergson's theory of dreaming here set forth in untechnical language, fits into a particular niche in his general system of philosophy as well as does his little book on *Laughter*. With the main features of his philosophy the English-reading public is better acquainted than with any other contemporary system, for his books have sold even more rapidly here than in France. When Professor Bergson visited the United States two years ago the lecture-rooms of Columbia University, like those of the Collège de France, were packed to the doors and the effect of his message was enhanced by his eloquence of delivery and charm of personality. The pragmatic character of his philosophy appeals to the genius of the American people as is shown by the influence of the teaching of William James and John Dewey, whose point of view in this respect resembles Bergson's.

During the present generation chemistry and biology have passed from the descriptive to the creative stage. Man is becoming the overlord of the mineral, vegetable and animal kingdoms. He is learning to make gems and perfumes, drugs and foods, to suit his tastes, instead of depending upon the chance bounty of nature. He is beginning consciously to adapt means to ends and to plan for the future even in the field of politics. He has opened up the atom and finds in it a microcosm more complex than the solar system. He beholds the elements melting with fervent heat and he turns their rays to the healing of his sores. He drives the lightning through the air and with the product feeds his crops. He makes the desert to blossom as the rose and out of the sea he draws forth dry land. He treats the earth as his habitation, remodeling it in accordance with his ever-varying needs and increasing ambitions.

This modern man, planning, contriving and making, finds Paley's watch as little to his mind as Lucretius's blind flow of atoms. A universe wound up once for all and doing nothing thereafter but mark time is as incomprehensible to him as a universe that never had a mind of its own and knows no difference between past and future. The idea of eternal recurrence does not frighten him as it did Nietzsche, for he feels it to be impossible. The mechanistic interpretation of natural phenomena developed during the last century he accepts at its full value, and would extend experimentally as far as it will go, for he finds it not invalid but inadequate.

To minds of this temperament it is no wonder that Bergson's *Creative Evolution* came with the force of an inspiration. Men felt themselves akin to this upward impulse, this *élan vital*, which, struggling throughout the ages with the intractableness of inert matter, yet finally in some way or other forces it to its will, and ever strives toward the increase of vitality, mentality, personality.

Bergson has been reluctant to commit himself on the question of immortality, but he of late has become quite convinced of it. He even goes so far as to think it possible that we may find experimental evidence of personal persistence after death. This at least we might infer from his recent acceptance of the presidency of the British Society for Psychical Research. In his opening address before the Society, May 28, 1913, he discussed the question of telepathy and in that connection he explained his theory of the relation of mind and brain in the following language. I quote from the report in the London *Times*:

The *rôle* of the brain is to bring back the remembrance of an action, to prolong the remembrance in movements. If one could see all that takes place in the interior of the brain, one would find that that which takes place there corresponds to a small part only of the life of the mind. The brain simply extracts from the life of the mind that which is capable of representation in movement. The cerebral life is to the mental life what the movements of the baton of a conductor are to the Symphony.

The brain, then, is that which allows the mind to adjust itself exactly to circumstances. It is the organ of attention to life. Should it become deranged, however slightly, the mind is no longer fitted to the circumstances; it wanders, dreams. Many forms of mental alienation are nothing else. But from this it results that one of the *rôles* of the brain is to limit the vision of the mind, to render its action more efficacious. This is what we observe in regard to the memory, where the *rôle* of the brain is to mask the useless part of our past in order to allow only the useful remembrances to appear. Certain useless recollections, or dream remembrances, manage nevertheless to appear also, and to form a vague fringe around the distinct recollections. It would not be at all surprising if perceptions of the organs of our senses, useful perceptions, were the result of a selection or of a canalization worked by the organs of our senses in the interest of our action, but that there should yet be around those perceptions a fringe of vague perceptions, capable of becoming more distinct in extraordinary, abnormal cases. Those would be precisely the cases with which psychical research would deal.

This conception of mental action forms, as will be seen, the foundation of the theory of dreams which Professor Bergson first presented in a lecture before the *Institut psychologique*, March 26, 1901. It was published in the *Revue scientifique* of June 8, 1901. An English translation, revised by the author and printed in *The Independent* of October 23 and 30, 1913, here appears for the first time in book form.

In this essay Professor Bergson made several contributions to our knowledge of dreams. He showed, in the first place, that dreaming is not so unlike the ordinary process of perception as had been hitherto supposed. Both use sense impressions as crude material to be molded and defined by the aid of memory images. Here, too, he set forth the idea, which he, so far as I know, was the first to formulate, that sleep is a state of disinterestedness, a theory which has since been adopted by several psychologists. In this address, also, was brought into consideration for the first time the idea that the self may go through different degrees of tension—a theory referred to in his *Matter and Memory*.

Its chief interest for the general reader will, however, lie in the explanation it gives him of the cause of some of his familiar dreams. He may by practice become the interpreter of his own visions and so come to an understanding of the vagaries of that mysterious and inseparable companion, his dream-self.

**Edwin E. Slosson.**

New York City,
February 10, 1914.

# DREAMS

The subject which I have to discuss here is so complex, it raises so many questions of all kinds, difficult, obscure, some psychological, others physiological and metaphysical; in order to be treated in a complete manner it requires such a long development—and we have so little space, that I shall ask your permission to dispense with all preamble, to set aside unessentials, and to go at once to the heart of the question.

A dream is this. I perceive objects and there is nothing there. I see men; I seem to speak to them and I hear what they answer; there is no one there and I have not spoken. It is all *as if* real things and real persons were there, then on waking all has disappeared, both persons and things. How does this happen?

But, first, is it true that there is nothing there? I mean, is there not presented a certain sense material to our eyes, to our ears, to our touch, etc., during sleep as well as during waking?

Close the eyes and look attentively at what goes on in the field of our vision. Many persons questioned on this point would say that nothing goes on, that they see nothing. No wonder at this, for a certain amount of practise is necessary to be able to observe oneself satisfactorily. But just give the requisite effort of attention, and you will distinguish, little by little, many things. First, in general, a black background. Upon this black background occasionally brilliant points which come and go, rising and descending, slowly and sedately. More often, spots of many colors, sometimes very dull, sometimes, on the contrary, with certain people, so brilliant that reality cannot compare with it. These spots spread and shrink, changing form and color, constantly displacing one another. Sometimes the change is slow and gradual, sometimes again it is a whirlwind of vertiginous rapidity. Whence comes all this phantasmagoria? The physiologists and the psychologists have studied this play of colors. "Ocular spectra," "colored spots," "phosphenes," such are the names that they have given to the phenomenon. They explain it either by the slight modifications which occur ceaselessly in the retinal circulation, or by the pressure that the closed lid exerts upon the eyeball, causing a mechanical excitation of the optic nerve. But the explanation of the phenomenon and the name that is given to it matters little. It occurs universally and it constitutes—I may say at once—the principal material of which we shape our dreams, "such stuff as dreams are made on."

Thirty or forty years ago, M. Alfred Maury and, about the same time, M. d'Hervey, of St. Denis, had observed that at the moment of falling asleep these colored spots and moving forms consolidate, fix themselves, take on definite outlines, the outlines of the objects and of the persons which people our dreams. But this is an observation to be accepted with caution, since it emanates from psychologists already half asleep. More recently an American psychologist, Professor Ladd, of Yale, has devised a more rigorous method, but of difficult application, because it requires a sort of training. It consists in acquiring the habit on awakening in the morning of keeping the eyes closed and retaining for some minutes the dream that is fading from the field of vision and soon would doubtless have faded from that of memory. Then one sees the figures and objects of the dream melt away little by little into phosphenes, identifying themselves with the colored spots that the eye really perceives when the lids are closed. One reads, for example, a newspaper; that is the dream. One awakens and there remains of the newspaper, whose definite outlines are erased, only a white spot with black marks here and there; that is the reality. Or our dream takes us upon the open sea—round about us the ocean spreads its waves of yellowish gray with here and there a crown of white foam. On awakening, it is all lost in a great spot, half yellow and half gray, sown with brilliant points. The spot was there, the brilliant points were there. There was really presented to our perceptions, in sleep, a visual dust, and it was this dust which served for the fabrication of our dreams.

Will this alone suffice? Still considering the sensation of sight, we ought to add to these visual sensations which we may call internal all those which continue to come to us from an external source. The eyes, when closed, still distinguish light from shade, and even, to a certain extent, different lights from one another. These sensations of light, emanating from without, are at the bottom of many of our dreams. A candle abruptly lighted in the room will, for example, suggest to the sleeper, if his slumber is not too deep, a dream dominated by the image of fire, the idea of a burning building. Permit me to cite to you two observations of M. Tissié on this subject:

"B—— Léon dreams that the theater of Alexandria is on *fire*; the flame lights up the whole place. All of a sudden he finds himself transported to the midst of the fountain in the public square; a line of *fire* runs along the chains which connect the great posts placed around the margin. Then he finds himself in Paris at the exposition, which is on *fire*. He takes part in terrible scenes, etc. He wakes with a start; his eyes catch the rays of light projected by the dark lantern which the night nurse flashes toward his bed in passing. M—— Bertrand dreams that he is in the marine infantry where he formerly served. He goes to Fort-de-France, to Toulon, to Loriet, to Crimea, to Constantinople. He sees lightning, he hears thunder, he takes part in a combat in which he sees *fire* leap from the mouths of cannon. He wakes with a start. Like B., he was wakened by a flash of light projected from the dark lantern of the night nurse." Such are often the dreams provoked by a bright and sudden light.

Very different are those which are suggested by a mild and continuous light like that of the moon. A. Krauss tells how one day on awakening he perceived that he was extending his arm toward what in his dream appeared to him to be the image of a young girl. Little by little this image melted into that of the full moon which darted its rays upon him. It is a curious thing that one might cite other examples of dreams where the rays of the moon, caressing the eyes of the sleeper, evoked before him virginal apparitions. May we not suppose that such might have been the origin in antiquity of the fable of Endymion— Endymion the shepherd, lapped in perpetual slumber, for whom the goddess Selene, that is, the moon, is smitten with love while he sleeps?

I have spoken of visual sensations. They are the principal ones. But the auditory sensations nevertheless play a rôle. First, the ear has also its internal sensations, sensations of buzzing, of tinkling, of whistling, difficult to isolate and to perceive while awake, but which are clearly distinguished in sleep. Besides that we continue, when once asleep, to hear external sounds. The creaking of furniture, the crackling of the fire, the rain beating against the window, the wind playing its chromatic scale in the chimney, such are the sounds which come to the ear of the sleeper and which the dream converts, according to circumstances, into conversation, singing, cries, music, etc. Scissors were struck against the tongs in the ears of Alfred Maury while he slept. Immediately he dreamt that he heard the tocsin and took part in the events of June, 1848. Such observations and experiences are numerous. But let us hasten to say that sounds do not play in our dreams so important a rôle as colors. Our dreams are, above all, visual, and even more visual than we think. To whom has it not happened—as M. Max Simon has remarked—to talk in a dream with a certain person, to dream a whole conversation, and then, all of a sudden, a singular phenomenon strikes the attention of the dreamer. He perceives that he does not speak, that he has not spoken, that his interlocutor has not uttered a single word, that it was a simple exchange of thought between them, a very clear conversation, in which, nevertheless, nothing has been heard. The phenomenon is easily enough explained. It is in general necessary for us to hear sounds in a dream. From nothing we can make nothing. And when we are not provided with sonorous material, a dream would find it hard to manufacture sonority.

There is much more to say about the sensations of touch than about those of hearing, but I must hasten. We could talk for hours about the singular phenomena which result from the confused sensations of touch during sleep. These sensations, mingling with the images which occupy our visual field, modify them or arrange them in their own way. Often in the midst of the night the contact of our body with its light clothing makes itself felt all at once and reminds us that we are lightly clothed. Then, if our dream is at the moment taking us through the street, it is in this simple attire that we present ourselves to the gaze of the passers-by, without their appearing to be astonished by it. We are ourselves astonished in the dream, but that never appears to astonish other people. I cite this dream because it is frequent. There is another which many of us must have experienced. It consists of feeling oneself flying through the air or floating in space. Once having had this dream, one may be quite sure that it will reappear; and every time that it recurs the dreamer reasons in this way: "I have had before now in a dream the illusion of flying or floating, but this time it is the real thing. It has certainly proved to me that we may free ourselves from the law of gravitation." Now, if you wake abruptly from this dream, you can analyze it without difficulty, if you undertake it immediately. You will see that you feel very clearly that your feet are not touching the earth. And, nevertheless, not believing yourself asleep, you have lost sight of the fact that you are lying down. Therefore, since you are not lying down and yet your feet do not feel the resistance of the ground, the conclusion is natural that you are floating in space. Notice this also: when levitation accompanies the flight, it is on one side only that you make an effort to fly. And if you woke at that moment you would find that this side is the one on which you are lying, and that the sensation of effort for flight coincides with the real sensation given you by the pressure of your body against the bed. This sensation of pressure, dissociated from its cause, becomes a pure and simple sensation of effort and, joined to the illusion of floating in space, is sufficient to produce the dream.

It is interesting to see that these sensations of pressure, mounting, so to speak, to the level of our visual field and taking advantage of the luminous dust which fills it, effect its transformation into forms and colors. M. Max Simon tells of having a strange and somewhat painful dream. He dreamt that he was confronted by two piles of golden coins, side by side and of unequal height, which for some reason or other he had to equalize. But he could not accomplish it. This produced a feeling of extreme anguish. This feeling, growing moment by moment, finally awakened him. He then perceived that one of his legs was caught by the folds of the bedclothes in such a way that his two feet were on different levels and it was impossible for him to bring them together. From this the sensation of inequality, making an irruption into the visual field and there encountering (such at least is the hypothesis which I propose) one or more yellow spots, expressed itself visually by the inequality of the two piles of gold pieces. There is, then, immanent in the tactile sensations during sleep, a tendency to visualize themselves and enter in this form into the dream.

More important still than the tactile sensations, properly speaking, are the sensations which pertain to what is sometimes called internal touch, deep-seated sensations emanating from all points of the organism and, more particularly, from the viscera. One cannot imagine the degree of sharpness, of acuity, which may be obtained during sleep by these interior sensations. They doubtless already exist as well during waking. But we are then distracted by practical action. We live outside of ourselves. But sleep makes us retire into ourselves. It happens frequently that persons subject to laryngitis, amygdalitis, etc., dream that they are attacked by their affection and experience a disagreeable tingling on the side of their throat. When awakened, they feel nothing more, and believe it an illusion; but a few hours later the illusion becomes a reality. There are cited maladies and grave accidents, attacks of epilepsy, cardiac affections, etc., which have been foreseen and, as it were, prophesied in dreams. We need not be astonished, then, that philosophers like Schopenhauer have seen in the dream a reverberation, in the heart of consciousness, of perturbations emanating from the sympathetic nervous system; and that psychologists like Schemer have attributed to each of our organs the power of provoking a well-determined kind of dream which represents it, as it were, symbolically; and finally that physicians like Artigues have written treatises on the semeiological value of dreams, that is to say, the method of making use of dreams for the diagnosis of certain maladies. More recently, M. Tissié, of whom we have just spoken, has shown how specific dreams are connected with affections of the digestive, respiratory, and circulatory apparatus.

I will summarize what I have just been saying. When we are sleeping naturally, it is not necessary to believe, as has often been supposed, that our senses are closed to external sensations. Our senses continue to be active. They act, it is true, with less precision, but in compensation they embrace a host of "subjective" impressions which pass unperceived when we are awake—for then we live in a world of perceptions common to all men—and which reappear in sleep, when we live only for ourselves. Thus our faculty of sense perception, far from being narrowed during sleep at all points, is on the contrary extended, at least in certain directions, in its field of operations. It is true that it often loses in energy, in *tension*, what it gains in extension. It brings to us only confused impressions. These impressions are the materials of our dreams. But they are only the materials, they do not suffice to produce them.

They do not suffice to produce them, because they are vague and indeterminate. To speak only of those that play the principal rôle, the changing colors and forms, which deploy before us when our eyes are closed, never have well-defined contours. Here are black lines upon a white background. They may represent to the dreamer the page of a book, or the facade of a new house with dark blinds, or any number of other things. Who will choose? What is the form that will imprint its decision upon the indecision of this material? This form is our memory.

Let us note first that the dream in general creates nothing. Doubtless there may be cited some examples of artistic, literary and scientific production in dreams. I will recall only the well-known anecdote told of Tartini, a violinist-composer of the eighteenth century. As he was trying to compose a sonata and the muse remained recalcitrant, he went to sleep and he saw in a dream the devil, who seized his violin and played with master hand the desired sonata. Tartini wrote it out from memory when he woke. It has come to us under the name of "The Devil's Sonata." But it is very difficult, in regard to such old cases, to distinguish between history and legend. We should have auto-observations of certain authenticity. Now I have not been able to find anything more than that of the contemporary English novelist, Stevenson. In a very curious essay entitled "A Chapter on Dreams," this author, who is endowed with a rare talent for analysis, explains to us how the most original of his stories have been composed or at least sketched in dreams. But read the chapter carefully. You will see that at a certain time in his life Stevenson had come to be in an habitual psychical state where it was very hard for him to say whether he was sleeping or waking. That appears to me to be the truth. When the mind creates, I would say when it is capable of giving the effort of organization and synthesis which is necessary to triumph over a certain difficulty, to solve a problem, to produce a living work of the imagination, we are not really asleep, or at least that part of ourselves which labors is not the same as that which sleeps. We cannot say, then, that it is a dream. In sleep, properly speaking, in sleep which absorbs our whole personality, it is memories and only memories which weave the web of our dreams. But often we do not recognize them. They may be very old memories, forgotten during waking hours, drawn from the most obscure depths of our past; they may be, often are, memories of objects that we have perceived distractedly, almost unconsciously, while awake. Or they may be fragments of broken memories which have been picked up here and there and mingled by chance, composing an incoherent and unrecognizable whole. Before these bizarre assemblages of images which present no plausible significance, our intelligence (which is far from surrendering the reasoning faculty during sleep, as has been asserted) seeks an explanation, tries to fill the lacunæ. It fills them by calling up other memories which, presenting themselves often with the same deformations and the same incoherences as the preceding, demand in their turn a new explanation, and so on indefinitely. But I do not insist upon this point for the moment. It is sufficient for me to say, in order to answer the question which I have propounded, that the formative power of the materials furnished to the dream by the different senses, the power which converts into precise, determined objects the vague and indistinct sensations that the dreamer receives from his eyes, his ears, and the whole surface and interior of his body, is the memory.

Memory! In a waking state we have indeed memories which appear and disappear, occupying our mind in turn. But they are always memories which are closely connected with our present situation, our present occupation, our present action. I recall at this moment the book of M. d'Hervey on dreams; that is because I am discussing the subject of dreams and this act orients in a certain particular direction the activity of my memory. The memories that we evoke while waking, however distant they may at first appear to be from the present action, are always connected with it in some way. What is the rôle of memory in an animal? It is to recall to him, in any circumstance, the advantageous or injurious consequences which have formerly arisen in analogous circumstances, in order to instruct him as to what he ought to do. In man memory is doubtless less the slave of action, but still it sticks to it. Our memories, at any given moment, form a solid whole, a pyramid, so to speak, whose point is inserted precisely into our present action. But behind the memories which are concerned in our occupations and are revealed by means of it, there are others, thousands of others, stored below the scene illuminated by consciousness. Yes, I believe indeed that all our past life is there, preserved even to the most infinitesimal details, and that we forget nothing, and that all that we have felt, perceived, thought, willed, from the first awakening of our consciousness, survives indestructibly. But the memories which are preserved in these obscure depths are there in the state of invisible phantoms. They aspire, perhaps, to the light, but they do not even try to rise to it; they know that it is impossible and that I, as a living and acting being, have something else to do than to occupy myself with them. But suppose that, at a given moment, I become *disinterested* in the present situation, in the present action—in short, in all which previously has fixed and guided my memory; suppose, in other words, that I am asleep. Then these memories, perceiving that I have taken away the obstacle, have raised the trapdoor which has kept them beneath the floor of consciousness, arise from the depths; they rise, they move, they perform in the night of unconsciousness a great dance macabre. They rush together to the door which has been left ajar. They all want to get through. But they cannot; there are too many of them. From the multitudes which are called, which will be chosen? It is not hard to say. Formerly, when I was awake, the memories which forced their way were those which could involve claims of relationship with the present situation, with what I saw and heard around me. Now it is more vague images which occupy my sight, more indecisive sounds which affect my ear, more indistinct touches which are distributed over the surface of my body, but there are also the more numerous sensations which arise from the deepest parts of the organism. So, then, among the phantom memories which aspire to fill themselves with color, with sonority, in short with materiality, the only ones that succeed are those which can assimilate themselves with the color-dust that we perceive, the external and internal sensations that we catch, etc., and which, besides, respond to the affective tone of our general sensibility.[1] When this union is effected between the memory and the sensation, we have a dream.

In a poetic page of the Enneades, the philosopher Plotinus, interpreter and continuator of Plato, explains to us how men come to life. Nature, he says, sketches the living bodies, but sketches them only. Left to her own forces she can never complete the task. On the other hand, souls inhabit the world of Ideas. Incapable in themselves of acting, not even thinking of action, they float beyond space and beyond time. But, among all the bodies, there are some which specially respond by their form to the aspirations of some particular souls; and among these souls there are those which recognize themselves in some particular body. The body, which does not come altogether viable from the hand of nature, rises toward the soul which might give it complete life; and the soul, looking upon the body and believing that it perceives its own image as in a mirror, and attracted, fascinated by the image, lets itself fall. It falls, and this fall is life. I may compare to these detached souls the memories plunged in the obscurity of the unconscious. On the other hand, our nocturnal sensations resemble these incomplete bodies. The sensation is warm, colored, vibrant and almost living, but vague. The memory is complete, but airy and lifeless. The sensation wishes to find a form on which to mold the vagueness of its contours. The memory would obtain matter to fill it, to ballast it, in short to realize it. They are drawn toward each other; and the phantom memory, incarnated in the sensation which brings to it flesh and blood, becomes a being with a life of its own, a dream.

The birth of a dream is then no mystery. It resembles the birth of all our perceptions. The mechanism of the dream is the same, in general, as that of normal perception. When we perceive a real object, what we actually see—the sensible matter of our perception—is very little in comparison with what our memory adds to it. When you read a book, when you look through your newspaper, do you suppose that all the printed letters really come into your consciousness? In that case the whole day would hardly be long enough for you to read a paper. The truth is that you see in each word and even in each member of a phrase only some letters or even some characteristic marks, just enough to permit you to divine the rest. All of the rest, that you think you see, you really give yourself as an hallucination. There are numerous and decisive experiments which leave no doubt on this point. I will cite only those of Goldscheider and Müller. These experimenters wrote or printed some formulas in common use, "Positively no admission;" "Preface to the fourth edition," etc. But they took care to write the words incorrectly, changing and, above all, omitting letters. These sentences were exposed in a darkened room. The person who served as the subject of the experiment was placed before them and did not know, of course, what had been written. Then the inscription was illuminated by the electric light for a very short time, too short for the observer to be able to perceive really all the letters. They began by determining experimentally the time necessary for seeing one letter of the alphabet. It was then easy to arrange it so that the observer could not perceive more than eight or ten letters, for example, of the thirty or forty letters composing the formula. Usually, however, he read the entire phrase without difficulty. But that is not for us the most instructive point of this experiment.

If the observer is asked what are the letters that he is sure of having seen, these may be, of course, the letters really written, but there may be also absent letters, either letters that we replaced by others or that have simply been omitted. Thus an observer will see quite distinctly in full light a letter which does not exist, if this letter, on account of the general sense, ought to enter into the phrase. The characters which have really affected the eye have been utilized only to serve as an indication to the unconscious memory of the observer. This memory, discovering the appropriate remembrance, *i.e.*, finding the formula to which these characters give a start toward realization, projects the remembrance externally in an hallucinatory form. It is this remembrance, and not the words themselves, that the observer has seen. It is thus demonstrated that rapid reading is in great part a work of divination, but not of abstract divination. It is an externalization of memories which take advantage, to a certain extent, of the partial realization that they find here and there in order to completely realize themselves.

Thus, in the waking state and in the knowledge that we get of the real objects which surround us, an operation is continually going on which is of quite the same nature as that of the dream. We perceive merely a sketch of the object. This sketch appeals to the complete memory, and this complete memory, which by itself was either unconscious or simply in the thought state, profits by the occasion to come out. It is this kind of hallucination, inserted and fitted into a real frame, that we perceive. It is a shorter process: it is very much quicker done than to see the thing itself. Besides, there are many interesting observations to be made upon the conduct and attitude of the memory images during this operation. It is not necessary to suppose that they are in our memory in a state of inert impressions. They are like the steam in a boiler, under more or less tension.

At the moment when the perceived sketch calls them forth, it is as if they were then grouped in families according to their relationship and resemblances. There are experiments of Münsterberg, earlier than those of Goldscheider and Müller, which appear to me to confirm this hypothesis, although they were made for a very different purpose. Münsterberg wrote the words correctly; they were, besides, not common phrases; they were isolated words taken by chance. Here again the word was exposed during the time too short for it to be entirely perceived. Now, while the observer was looking at the written word, some one spoke in his ear another word of a very different significance. This is what happened: the observer declared that he had seen a word which was not the written word, but which resembled it in its general form, and which besides recalled, by its meaning, the word which was spoken in his ear. For example, the word written was "tumult" and the word spoken was "railroad." The observer read "tunnel." The written word was "Trieste" and the spoken word was the German "Verzweiflung" (despair). The observer read "Trost," which signifies "consolation." It is as if the word "railroad," pronounced in the ear, wakened, without our knowing it, hopes of conscious realization in a crowd of memories which have some relationship with the idea of "railroad" (car, rail, trip, etc.). But this is only a hope, and the memory which succeeds in coming into consciousness is that which the actually present sensation had already begun to realize.

Such is the mechanism of true perception, and such is that of the dream. In both cases there are, on one hand, real impressions made upon the organs of sense, and upon the other memories which encase themselves in the impression and profit by its vitality to return again to life.

But, then, what is the essential difference between perceiving and dreaming? What is sleep? I do not ask, of course, how sleep can be explained physiologically. That is a special question, and besides is far from being settled. I ask what is sleep psychologically; for our mind continues to exercise itself when we are asleep, and it exercises itself as we have just seen on elements analogous to those of waking, on sensations and memories; and also in an analogous manner combines them. Nevertheless we have on the one hand normal perception, and on the other the dream. What is the difference, I repeat? What are the psychological characteristics of the sleeping state?

We must distrust theories. There are a great many of them on this point. Some say that sleep consists in isolating oneself from the external world, in closing the senses to outside things. But we have shown that our senses continue to act during sleep, that they provide us with the outline, or at least the point of departure, of most of our dreams. Some say: "To go to sleep is to stop the action of the superior faculties of the mind," and they talk of a kind of momentary paralysis of the higher centers. I do not think that this is much more exact. In a dream we become no doubt *indifferent* to logic, but not *incapable* of logic. There are dreams when we reason with correctness and even with subtlety. I might almost say, at the risk of seeming paradoxical, that the mistake of the dreamer is often in reasoning too much. He would avoid the absurdity if he would remain a simple spectator of the procession of images which compose his dream. But when he strongly desires to explain it, his explanation, intended to bind together incoherent images, can be nothing more than a bizarre reasoning which verges upon absurdity. I recognize, indeed, that our superior intellectual faculties are relaxed in sleep, that generally the logic of a dreamer is feeble enough and often resembles a mere parody of logic. But one might say as much of all of our faculties during sleep. It is then not by the abolition of reasoning, any more than by the closing of the senses, that we characterize dreaming.

Something else is essential. We need something more than theories. We need an intimate contact with the facts. One must make the decisive experiment upon oneself. It is necessary that on coming out of a dream, since we cannot analyze ourselves in the dream itself, we should watch the transition from sleeping to waking, follow upon the transition as closely as possible, and try to express by words what we experience in this passage. This is very difficult, but may be accomplished by forcing the attention. Permit, then, the writer to take an example from his own personal experience, and to tell of a recent dream as well as what was accomplished on coming out of the dream.

Now the dreamer dreamed that he was speaking before an assembly, that he was making a political speech before a political assembly. Then in the midst of the auditorium a murmur rose. The murmur augmented; it became a muttering. Then it became a roar, a frightful tumult, and finally there resounded from all parts timed to a uniform rhythm the cries, "Out! Out!" At that moment he wakened. A dog was baying in a neighboring garden, and with each one of his "Wow-wows" one of the cries of "Out! Out!" seemed to be identical. Well, here was the infinitesimal moment which it is necessary to seize.

The waking ego, just reappearing, should turn to the dreaming ego, which is still there, and, during some instants at least, hold it without letting it go. "I have caught you at it! You thought it was a crowd shouting and it was a dog barking. Now, I shall not let go of you until you tell me just what you were doing!" To which the dreaming ego would answer, "I was doing nothing; and this is just where you and I differ from one another. You imagine that in order to hear a dog barking, and to know that it is a dog that barks, you have nothing to do. That is a great mistake. You accomplish, without suspecting it, a considerable effort. You take your entire memory, all your accumulated experience, and you bring this formidable mass of memories to converge upon a single point, in such a way as to insert exactly in the sounds you heard that one of your memories which is the most capable of being adapted to it. Nay, you must obtain a perfect adherence, for between the memory that you evoke and the crude sensation that you perceive there must not be the least discrepancy; otherwise you would be just dreaming. This adjustment you can only obtain by an effort of the memory and an effort of the perception, just as the tailor who is trying on a new coat pulls together the pieces of cloth that he adjusts to the shape of your body in order to pin them. You exert, then, continually, every moment of the day, an enormous effort. Your life in a waking state is a life of labor, even when you think you are doing nothing, for at every minute you have to choose and every minute exclude. You choose among your sensations, since you reject from your consciousness a thousand subjective sensations which come back in the night when you sleep. You choose, and with extreme precision and delicacy, among your memories, since you reject all that do not exactly suit your present state. This choice which you continually accomplish, this adaptation, ceaselessly renewed, is the first and most essential condition of what is called common sense. But all this keeps you in a state of uninterrupted tension. You do not feel it at the moment, any more than you feel the pressure of the atmosphere, but it fatigues you in the long run. Common sense is very fatiguing.

"So, I repeat, I differ from you precisely in that I do nothing. The effort that you give without cessation I simply abstain from giving. In place of attaching myself to life, I detach myself from it. Everything has become indifferent to me. I have become disinterested in everything. To sleep is to become disinterested. One sleeps to the exact extent to which he becomes disinterested. A mother who sleeps by the side of her child will not stir at the sound of thunder, but the sigh of the child will wake her. Does she really sleep in regard to her child? We do not sleep in regard to what continues to interest us.

"You ask me what it is that I do when I dream? I will tell you what you do when you are awake. You take me, the me of dreams, me the totality of your past, and you force me, by making me smaller and smaller, to fit into the little circle that you trace around your present action. That is what it is to be awake. That is what it is to live the normal psychical life. It is to battle. It is to will. As for the dream, have you really any need that I should explain it? It is the state into which you naturally fall when you let yourself go, when you no longer have the power to concentrate yourself upon a single point, when you have ceased to will. What needs much more to be explained is the marvelous mechanism by which at any moment your will obtains instantly, and almost unconsciously, the concentration of all that you have within you upon one and the same point, the point that interests you. But to explain this is the task of normal psychology, of the psychology of waking, for willing and waking are one and the same thing."

This is what the dreaming ego would say. And it would tell us a great many other things still if we could let it talk freely. But let us sum up briefly the essential difference which separates a dream from the waking state. In the dream the same faculties are exercised as during waking, but they are in a state of tension in the one case, and of relaxation in the other. The dream consists of the entire mental life minus the tension, the effort and the bodily movement. We perceive still, we remember still, we reason still. All this can abound in the dream; for abundance, in the domain of the mind, does not mean effort. What requires an effort is the precision of adjustment. To connect the sound of a barking dog with the memory of a crowd that murmurs and shouts requires no effort. But in order that this sound should be perceived as the barking of a dog, a positive effort must be made. It is this force that the dreamer lacks. It is by that, and by that alone, that he is distinguished from the waking man.

From this essential difference can be drawn a great many others. We can come to understand the chief characteristics of the dream. But I can only outline the scheme of this study. It depends especially upon three points, which are: the incoherence of dreams, the abolition of the sense of duration that often appears to be manifested in dreams, and, finally, the order in which the memories present themselves to the dreamer, contending for the sensations present where they are to be embodied.

The incoherence of the dream seems to me easy enough to explain. As it is characteristic of the dream not to demand a complete adjustment between the memory image and the sensation, but, on the contrary, to allow some play between them, very different memories can suit the same sensation. For example, there may be in the field of vision a green spot with white points. This might be a lawn spangled with white flowers. It might be a billiard-table with its balls. It might be a host of other things besides. These different memory images, all capable of utilizing the same sensation, chase after it. Sometimes they attain it, one after the other. And so the lawn becomes a billiard-table, and we watch these extraordinary transformations. Often it is at the same time, and altogether that these memory images join the sensation, and then the lawn will be a billiard-table. From this come those absurd dreams where an object remains as it is and at the same time becomes something else. As I have just said, the mind, confronted by these absurd visions, seeks an explanation and often thereby aggravates the incoherence.

As for the abolition of the sense of time in many of our dreams, that is another effect of the same cause. In a few seconds a dream can present to us a series of events which will occupy, in the waking state, entire days. You know the example cited by M. Maury: it has become classic, and although it has been contested of late, I regard it as probable, because of the great number of analogous observations that I found scattered through the literature of dreams. But this precipitation of the images is not at all mysterious. When we are awake we live a life in common with our fellows. Our attention to this external and social life is the great regulator of the succession of our internal states. It is like the balance wheel of a watch, which moderates and cuts into regular sections the undivided, almost instantaneous tension of the spring. It is this balance wheel which is lacking in the dream. Acceleration is no more than abundance a sign of force in the domain of the mind. It is, I repeat, the precision of adjustment that requires effort, and this is exactly what the dreamer lacks. He is no longer capable of that attention to life which is necessary in order that the inner may be regulated by the outer, and that the internal duration fit exactly into the general duration of things.

It remains now to explain how the peculiar relaxation of the mind in the dream accounts for the preference given by the dreamer to one memory image rather than others, equally capable of being inserted into the actual sensations. There is a current prejudice to the effect that we dream mostly about the events which have especially preoccupied us during the day. This is sometimes true. But when the psychological life of the waking state thus prolongs itself into sleep, it is because we hardly sleep. A sleep filled with dreams of this kind would be a sleep from which we come out quite fatigued. In normal sleep our dreams concern themselves rather, other things being equal, with the thoughts which we have passed through rapidly or upon objects which we have perceived almost without paying attention to them. If we dream about events of the same day, it is the most insignificant facts, and not the most important, which have the best chance of reappearing.

I agree entirely on this point with the observation of W. Robert, of Delage and of Freud. I was in the street, I was waiting for a street-car, I stood beside the track and did not run the least risk. But if, at the moment when the street-car passed, the idea of possible danger had crossed my mind or even if my body had instinctively recoiled without my having been conscious of feeling any fear, I might dream that night that the car had run over my body. I watch at the bedside of an invalid whose condition is hopeless. If at any moment, perhaps without even being aware of it, I had hoped against hope, I might dream that the invalid was cured. I should dream of the cure, in any case, more probably than that I should dream of the disease. In short, the events which reappear by preference in the dream are those of which we have thought most distractedly. What is there astonishing about that? The ego of the dream is an ego that is relaxed; the memories which it gathers most readily are the memories of relaxation and distraction, those which do not bear the mark of effort.

It is true that in very profound slumber the law that regulates the reappearance of memories may be very different. We know almost nothing of this profound slumber. The dreams which fill it are, as a general rule, the dreams which we forget. Sometimes, nevertheless, we recover something of them. And then it is a very peculiar feeling, strange, indescribable, that we experience. It seems to us that we have returned from afar in space and afar in time. These are doubtless very old scenes, scenes of youth or infancy that we live over then in all their details, with a mood which colors them with that fresh sensation of infancy and youth that we seek vainly to revive when awake.

It is upon this profound slumber that psychology ought to direct its efforts, not only to study the mechanism of unconscious memory, but to examine the more mysterious phenomena which are raised by "psychical research." I do not dare express an opinion upon phenomena of this class, but I cannot avoid attaching some importance to the observations gathered by so rigorous a method and with such indefatigable zeal by the Society for Psychical Research. If telepathy influences our dreams, it is quite likely that in this profound slumber it would have the greatest chance to manifest itself. But I repeat, I cannot express an opinion upon this point. I have gone forward with you as far as I can; I stop upon the threshold of the mystery. To explore the most secret depths of the unconscious, to labor in what I have just called the subsoil of consciousness, that will be the principal task of psychology in the century which is opening. I do not doubt that wonderful discoveries await it there, as important perhaps as have been in the preceding centuries the discoveries of the physical and natural sciences. That at least is the promise which I make for it, that is the wish that in closing I have for it.

## FOOTNOTES:

[1] Author's note (1913). This would be the place where especially will intervene those "repressed desires" which Freud and certain other psychologists, especially in America, have studied with such penetration and ingenuity. (See in particular the recent volumes of the *Journal of Abnormal Psychology*, published in Boston by Dr. Morton Prince.) When the above address was delivered (1901) the work of Freud on dreams (*Die Traumdeutung*) had been already published, but "psycho-analysis" was far from having the development that it has to-day. (H. B.)

Made in the USA
Middletown, DE
20 August 2016